COLDPLAY

VIVA LA VIDA

OR

DEATH AND ALL HIS FRIENDS

Music arranged by Matt Cowe.
Music processed by Paul Ewers Music Design.
Edited by Tom Farncombe.

With special thanks to Arthur Dick.

Cover painting by Eugéne Delacroix.
Original CD design by Tappin Gofton.
Photography by Dan Green and Guy Berryman.

ISBN: 978-1-4234-6071-8

HAL•LEONARD®
CORPORATION
7777 W. BLUEMOUND RD. P.O. BOX 13819 MILWAUKEE, WI 53213

Printed in the EU.

Visit Hal Leonard Online at
www.halleonard.com

Life In Technicolor

Words & Music by
Guy Berryman, Chris Martin, Jon Buckland, Will Champion & Jon Hopkins

Cemeteries Of London

Words & Music by
Guy Berryman, Chris Martin, Jon Buckland & Will Champion

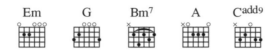

To match original recording tune guitars down 1 semitone

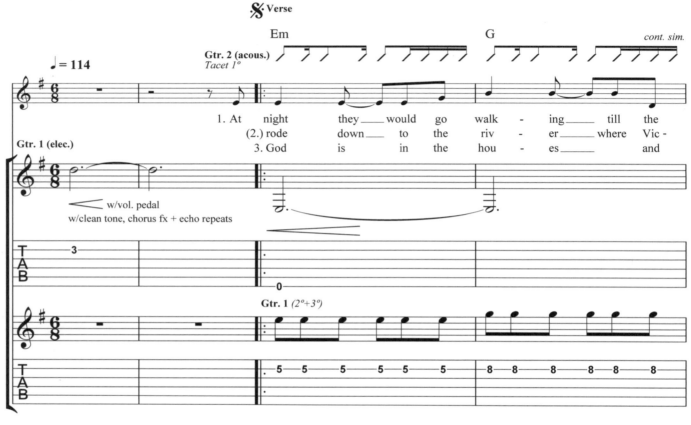

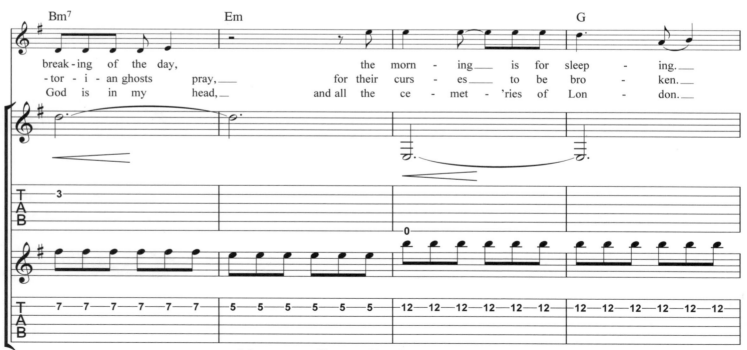

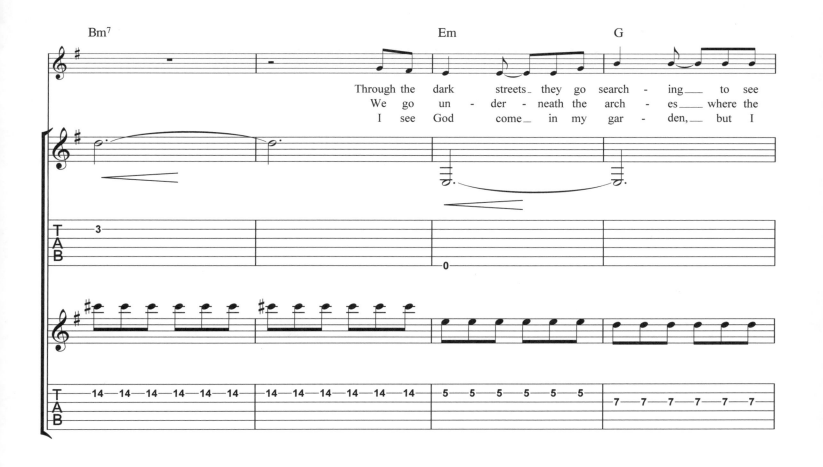

Through the dark streets they go search - ing__ to see
We go un - der - neath the arch - es__ where the
I see God come__ in my gar - den,__ but I

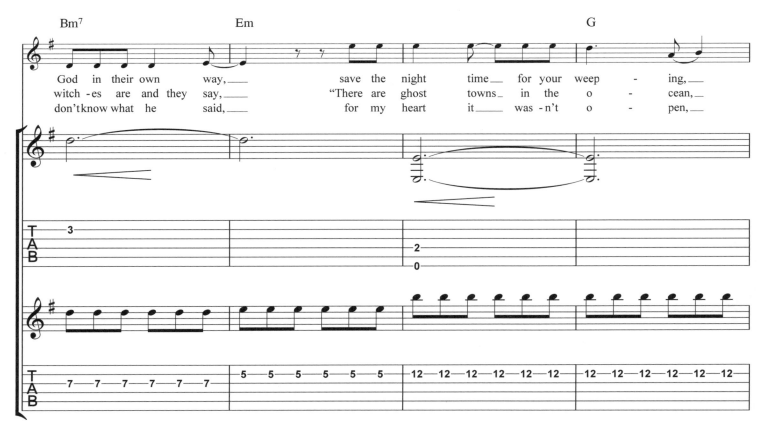

God in their own way,__ save the night time__ for your weep - ing,__
witch - es are and they say,__ "There are ghost towns__ in the o - cean,
don't know what he said,__ for my heart it__ was - n't o - pen,

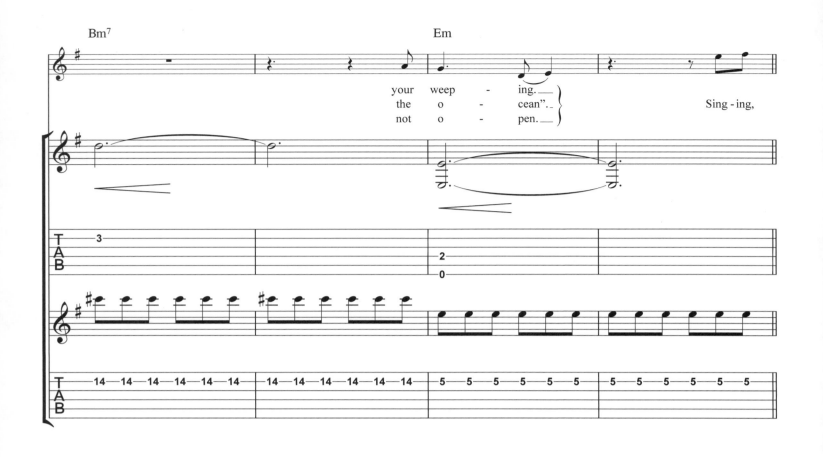

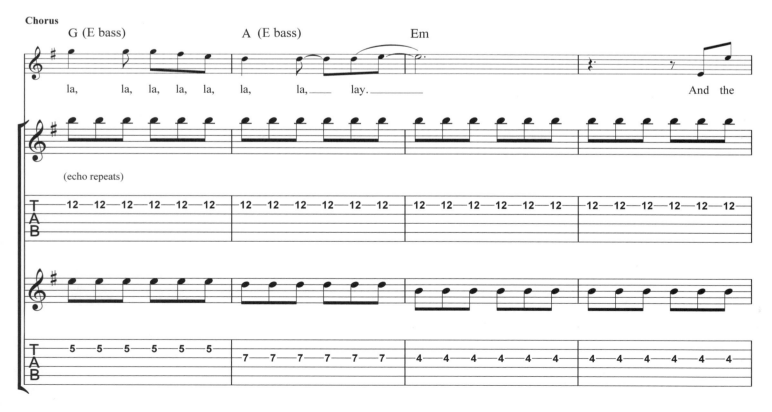

LOST!

WORDS & MUSIC BY
GUY BERRYMAN, CHRIS MARTIN, JON BUCKLAND & WILL CHAMPION

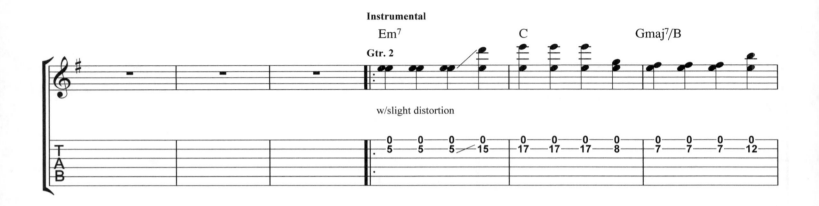

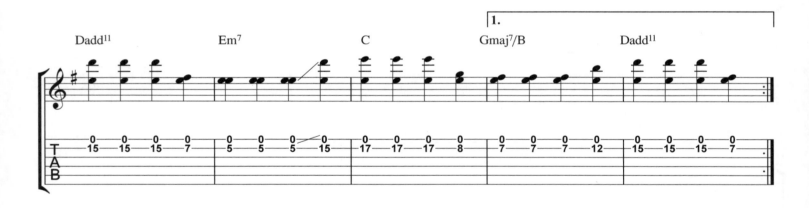

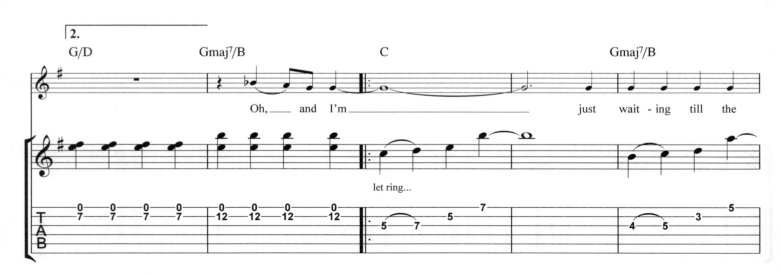

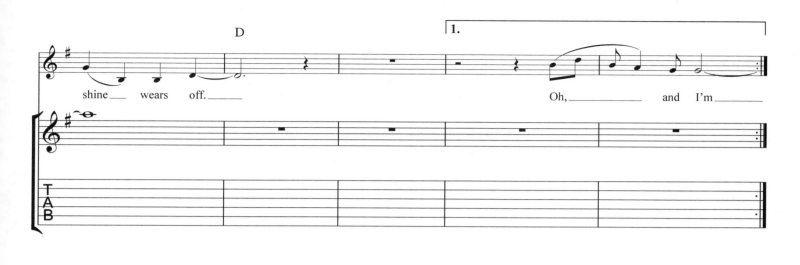

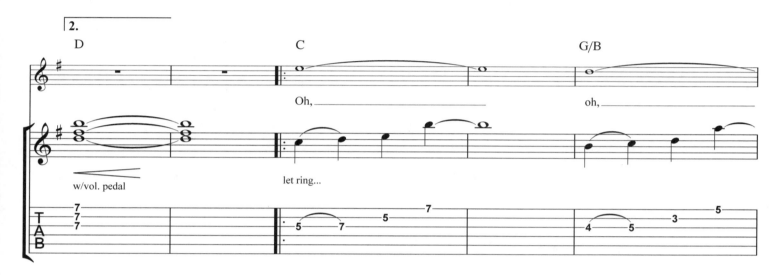

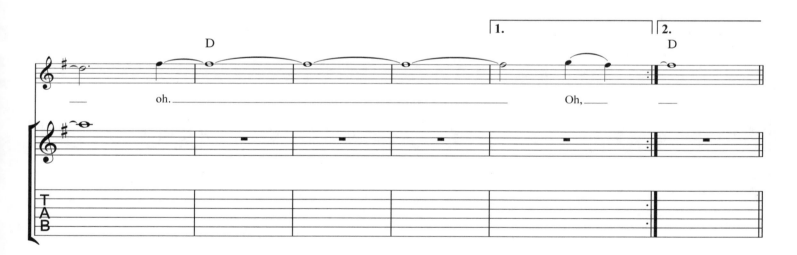

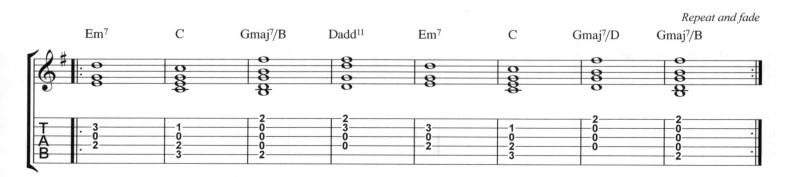

42

WORDS & MUSIC BY
GUY BERRYMAN, CHRIS MARTIN, JON BUCKLAND & WILL CHAMPION

Time is___ so short___ and I'm sure___ there must___ be some-thing more.___

Oh.___

Strings arr. for Gtr.

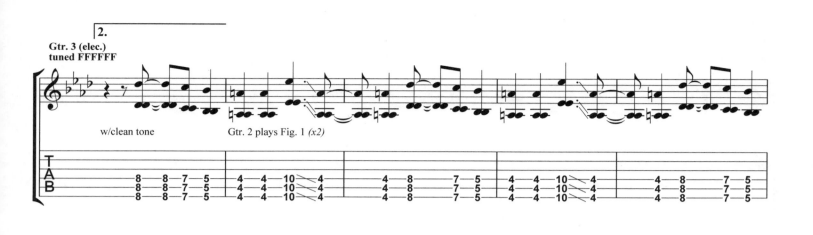

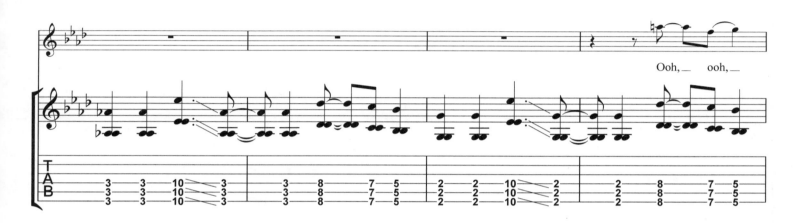

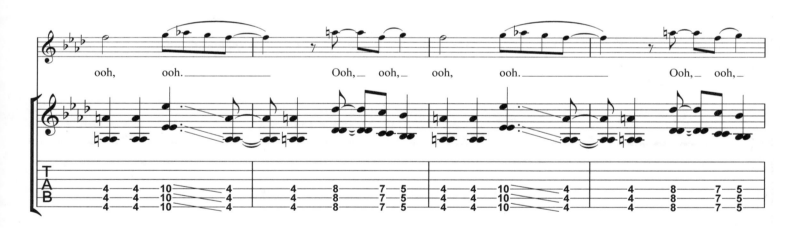

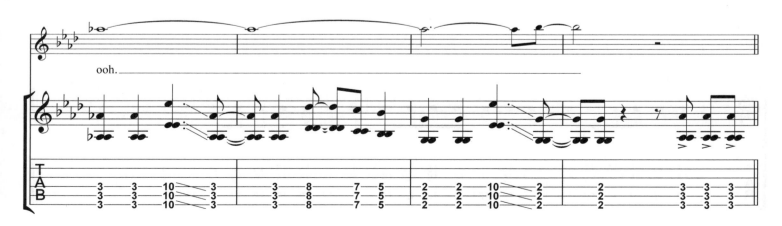

Those who are dead are not dead, they're just liv-ing in ___ my head.

Oh, ___ oh.

head.

Ooh. ___

Lovers In Japan

Words & Music by
Guy Berryman, Chris Martin, Jon Buckland & Will Champion

31

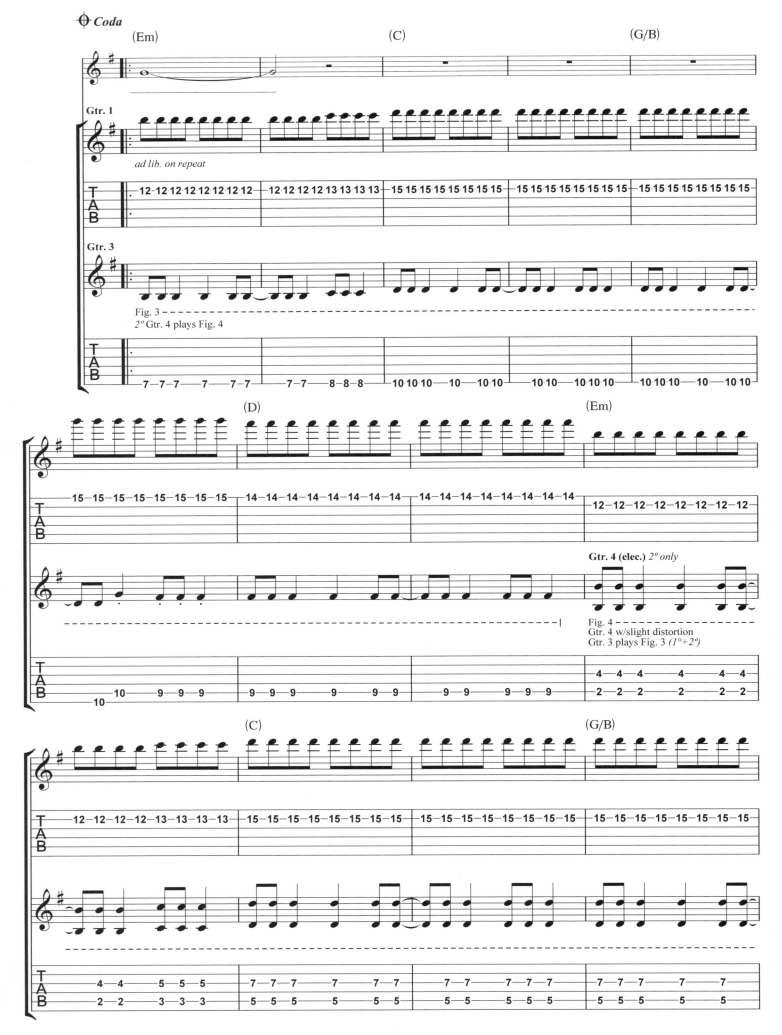

Reign Of Love

Words & Music by
Guy Berryman, Chris Martin, Jon Buckland & Will Champion

Verse

1. Reign of of___ love,___ I can't let___ go.___
2. *Instrumental until* *
3. Reign of___ love,___ by the church, we're wait - ing.
4. *Instrumental*

___ To the sea___ I of - - - fer this
Reign of___ love,___ on my

35

Yes

WORDS & MUSIC BY
GUY BERRYMAN, CHRIS MARTIN, JON BUCKLAND & WILL CHAMPION

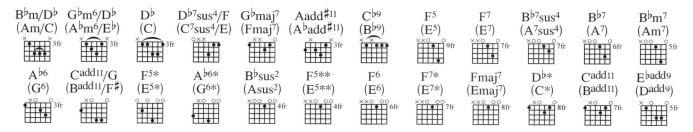

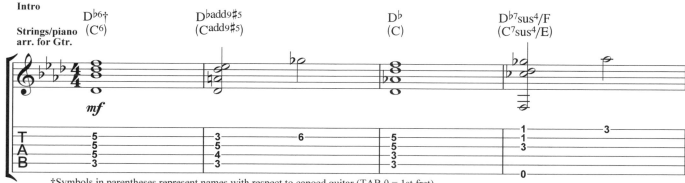

♩ = 164 With half-time feel

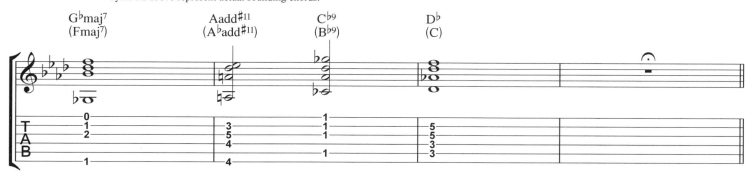

†Symbols in parentheses represent names with respect to capoed guitar (TAB 0 = 1st fret).
Symbols above represent actual sounding chords.

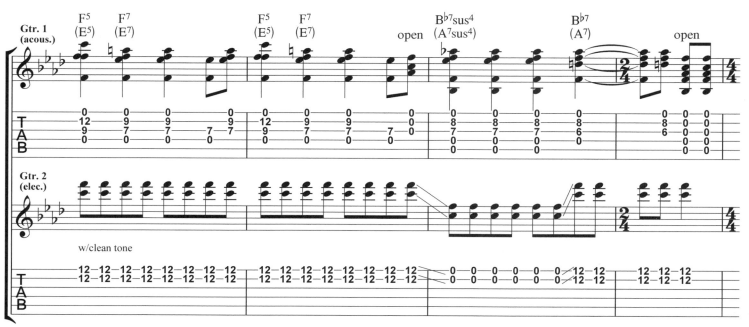

39

40

Chinese Sleep Chant

Words & Music by
Guy Berryman, Chris Martin, Jon Buckland & Will Champion

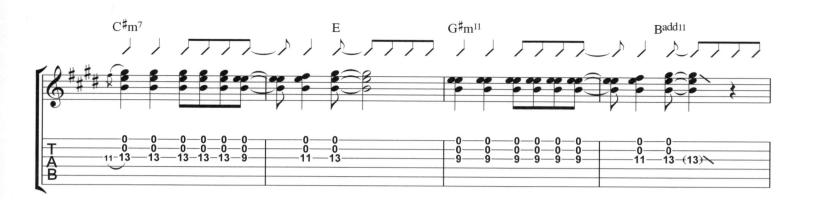

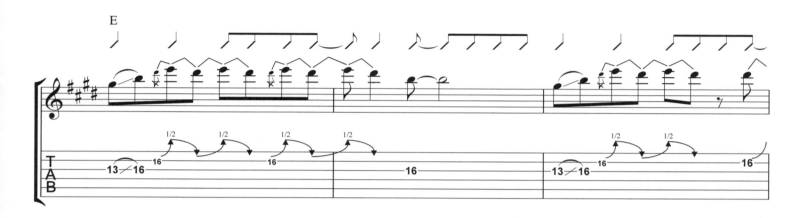

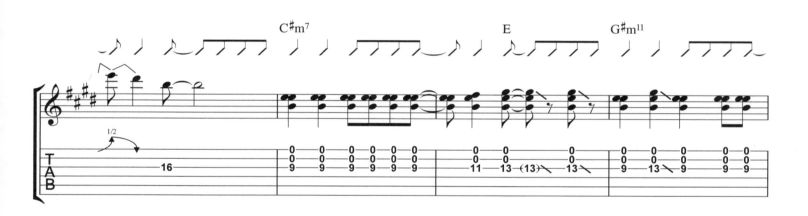

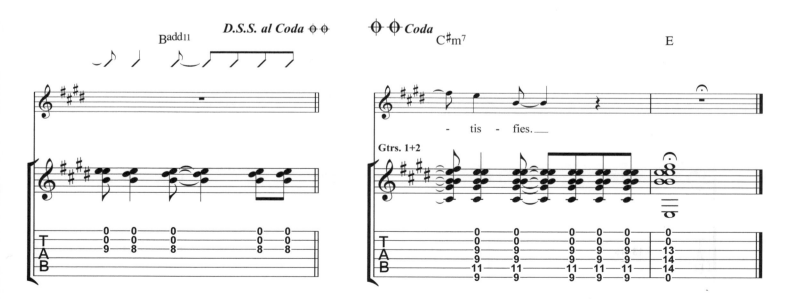

Viva La Vida

Words & Music by
Guy Berryman, Chris Martin, Jon Buckland & Will Champion

†Symbols in parentheses represent names with respect to capoed guitar (TAB 0 = 1st fret).
Symbols above represent actual sounding chords.

rule the world,___ seas would rise when I gave___ the word. Now in the morn-ing I

Gtr. 1 w/Fig. 1 (x4)

sleep a-lone,___ sweep the streets I used to own.___

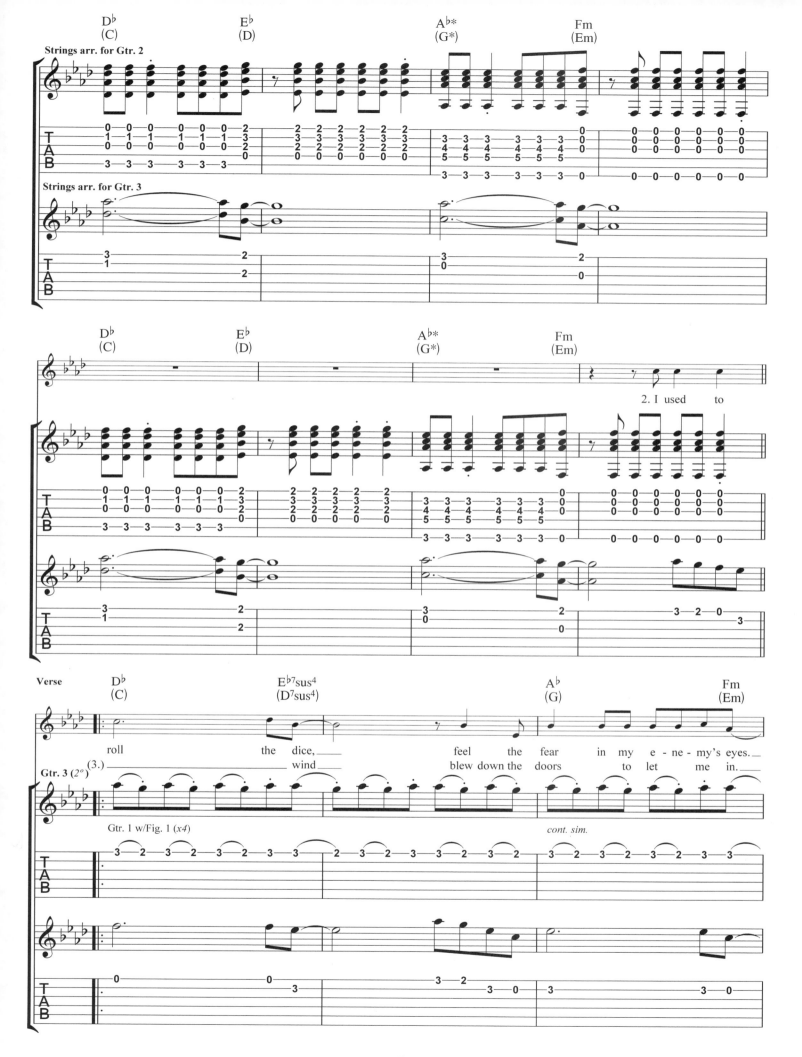

50

cas - tles stand____ up - on pil - lars of salt__ and pil - lars of sand. I
lone - ly string,____ oh, who would ev - er want to be king?____ I

Chorus

hear Je - ru - sa - lem bells____ a - ring - ing, Ro - man Ca - val - ry choirs____ are sing - ing.
(𝄋) hear Je - ru - sa - lem bells____ a - ring - ing, Ro - man Ca - val - ry choirs____ are sing - ing.

f Gtr. 1 w/Fig. 1 (x4)

Be my mir - ror, my sword____ and shield,____ my mis - sio - na - ries in a for - eign field.____
Be my mir - ror, my sword____ and shield,____ my mis - sio - na - ries in a for - eign field.____

For some rea - son I can't____ ex - plain,__ once you'd gone there was ne - ver, ne - ver an hon -
For some rea - son I can't____ ex - plain,__ I know Saint Pe - ter won't call____ my name. Ne - ver

To Coda ⊕

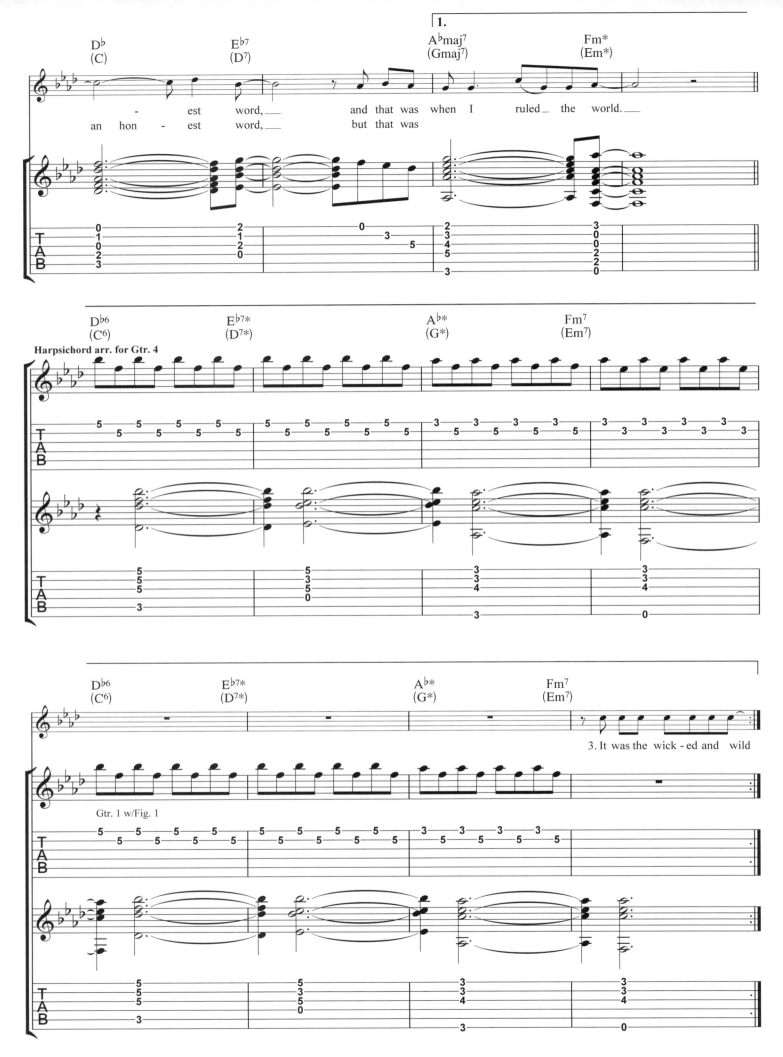

est word, ___ and that was when I ruled ___ the world. ___
an hon - est word, ___ but that was

3. It was the wick - ed and wild

Violet Hill

Words & Music by
Guy Berryman, Chris Martin, Jon Buckland & Will Champion

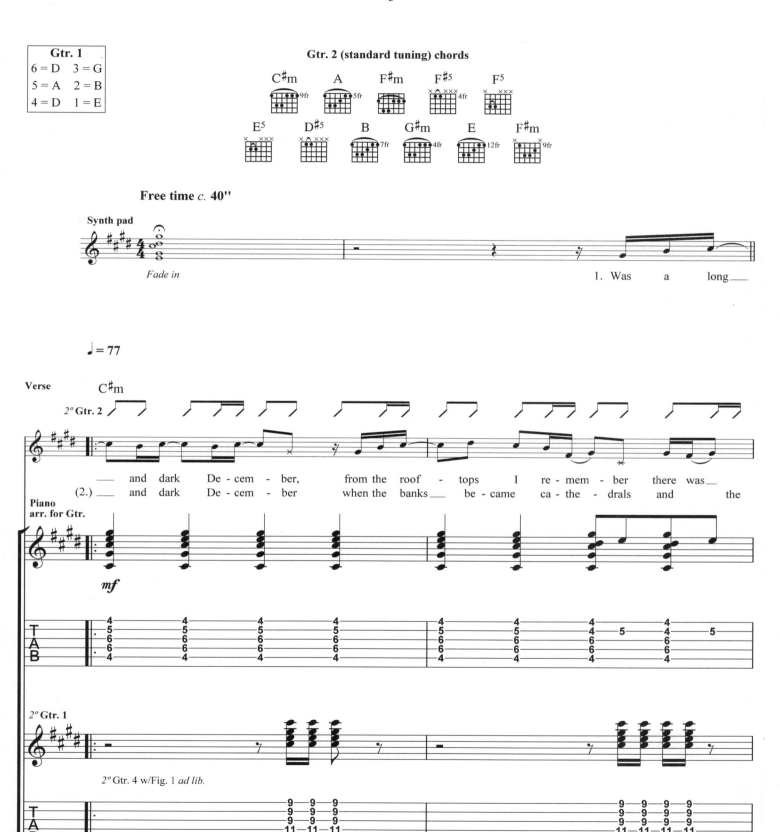

snow, white snow. Clear-
fox be - came God. Priests

_1°+2°_ **Gtr. 1 (elec.), tuned DADGBE**

w/distortion

_1°+2°_
Gtr. 2 (acous.)

- ly I_ re - mem - ber from the win - dow they were watch - ing while we
_ clutched on to bi - bles hollowed out_ to fit_ their ri - fles and the

_2°_ **Gtr. 1**

froze_ down be - low._ When the fu-
cross_ was held a - loft._ Bu-

_1°+2°_ **Gtr. 1**

Coda

I took my love down to Vio - let Hill, there we sat

— in snow. All that time she was si - lent still. So, if you love me won't you

let me know. If you love me, won't you let me know.

Strawberry Swing

Words & Music by
Guy Berryman, Chris Martin, Jon Buckland & Will Champion

†Symbols in parentheses represent names with respect to capoed guitar.
Symbols above represent actual sounding chords.

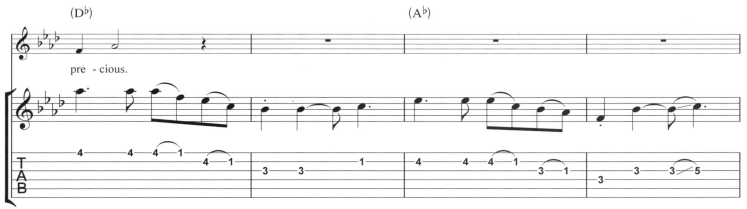

such a per - fect day.

It's such a per - fect day.

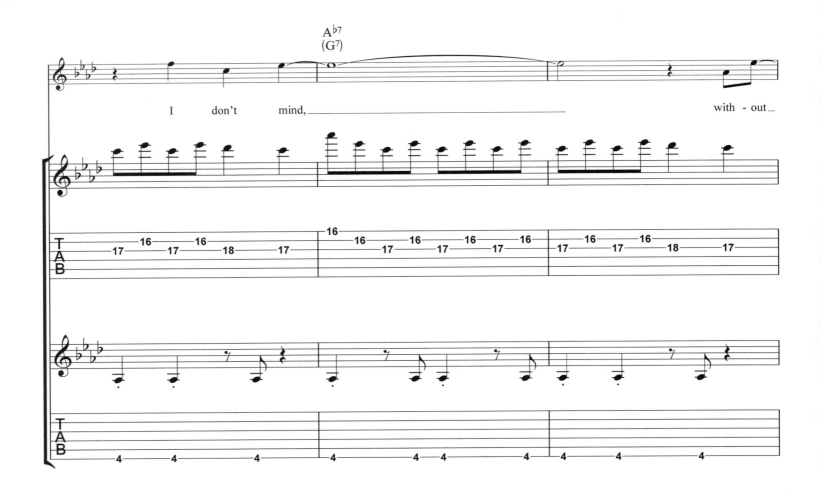

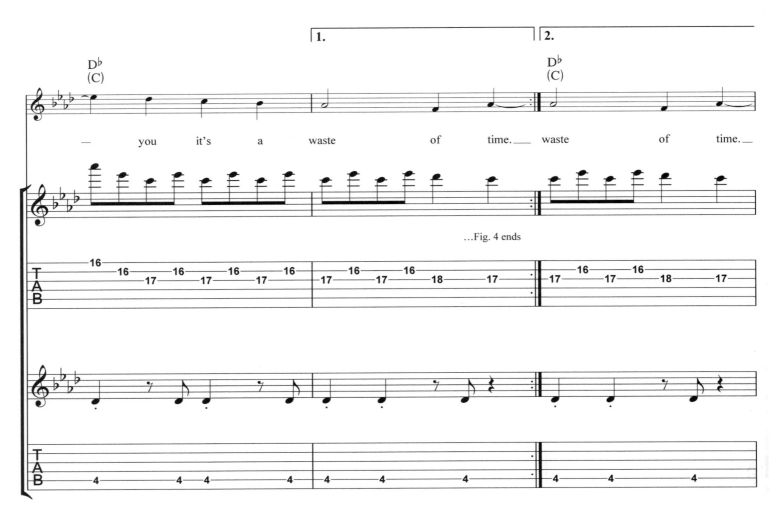

DEATH AND ALL HIS FRIENDS

WORDS & MUSIC BY
GUY BERRYMAN, CHRIS MARTIN, JON BUCKLAND & WILL CHAMPION

sum - mer we just hur - - ied, _____ so come o-

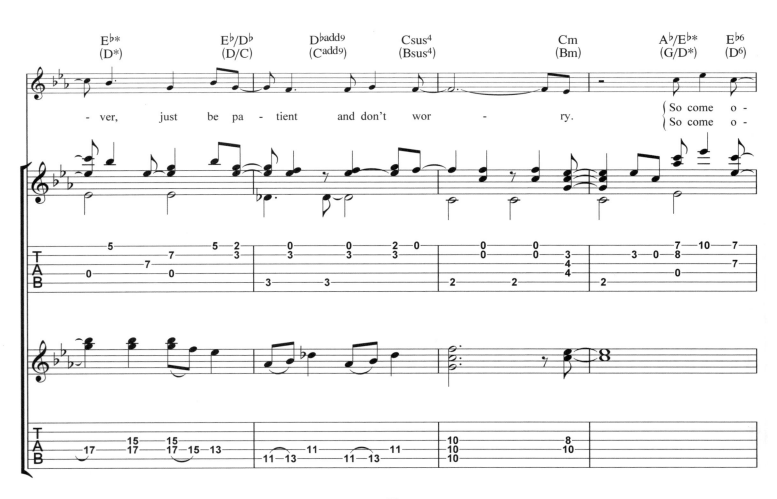

- ver, just be pa - tient and don't wor - ry.

So come o-
So come o-

70

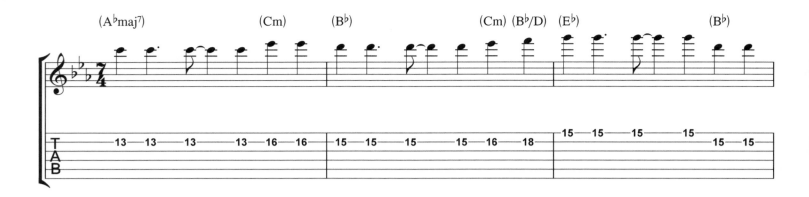

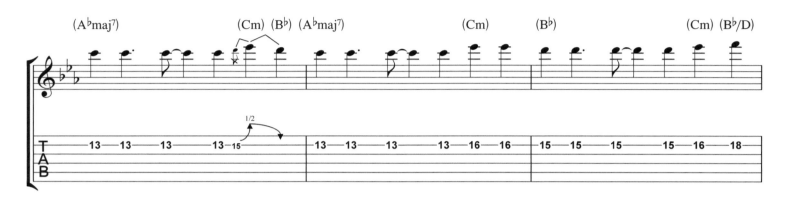

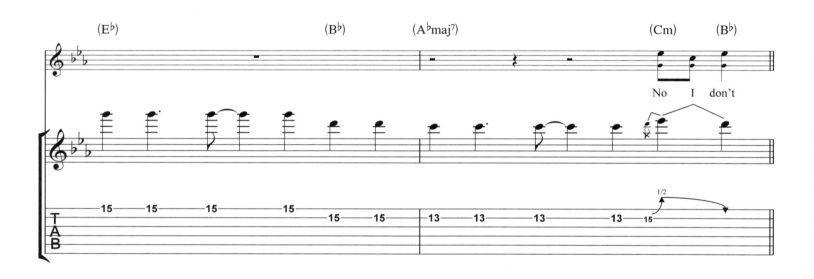

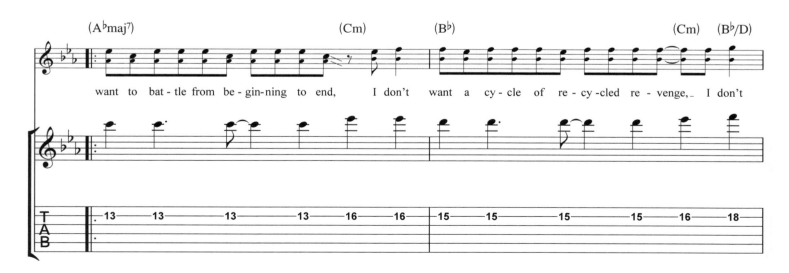

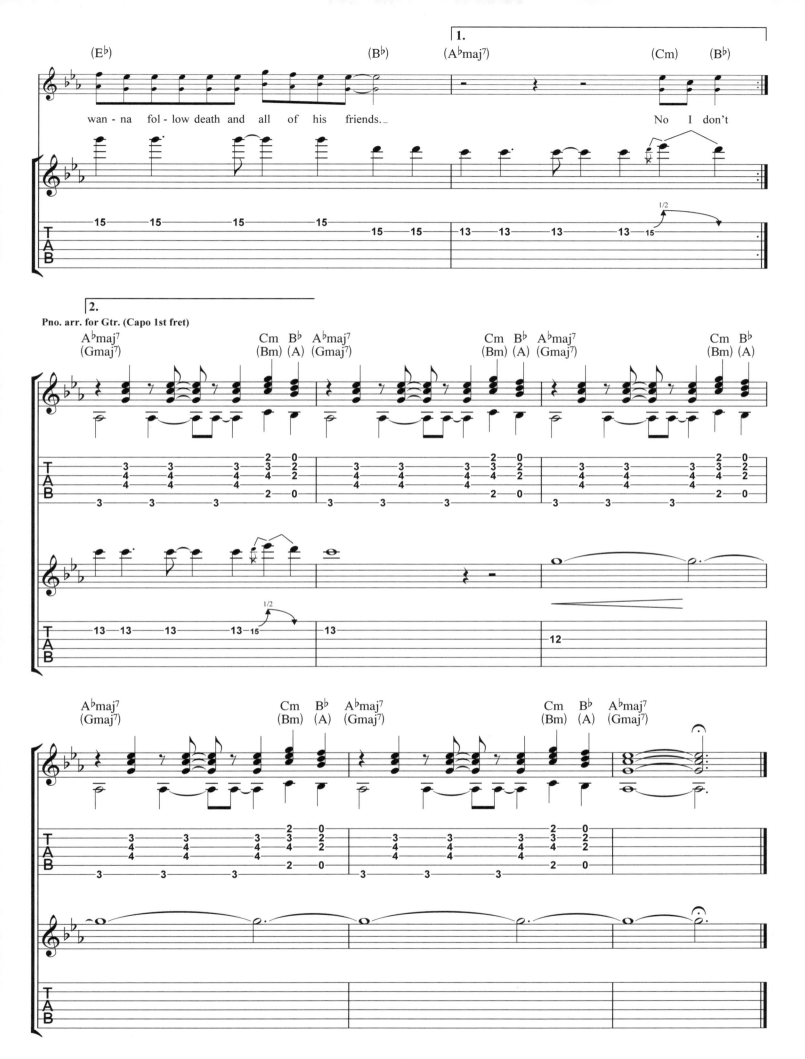

The Escapist

Words & Music by
Guy Berryman, Chris Martin, Jon Buckland, Will Champion & Jon Hopkins

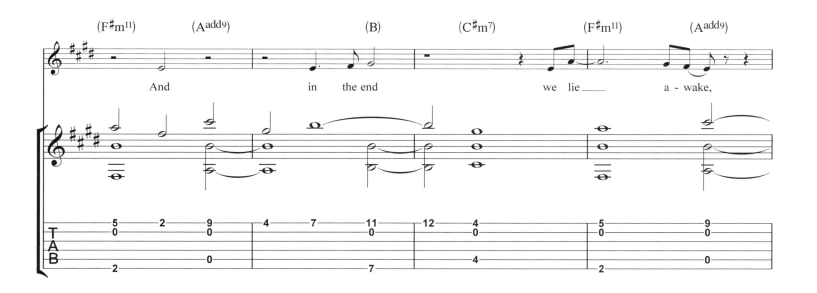

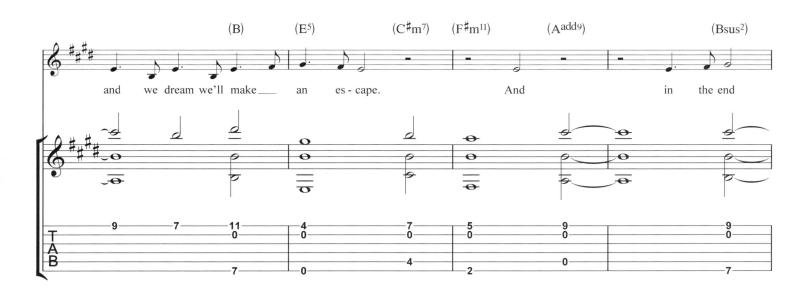

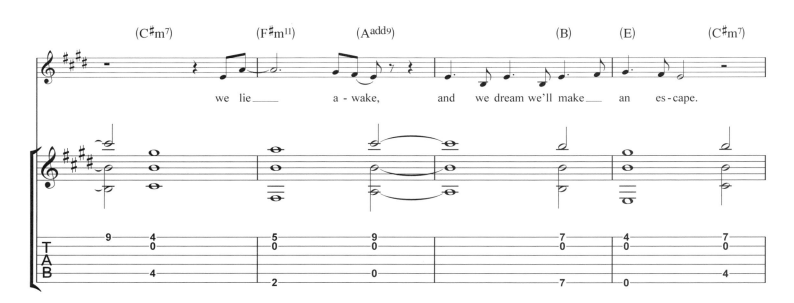

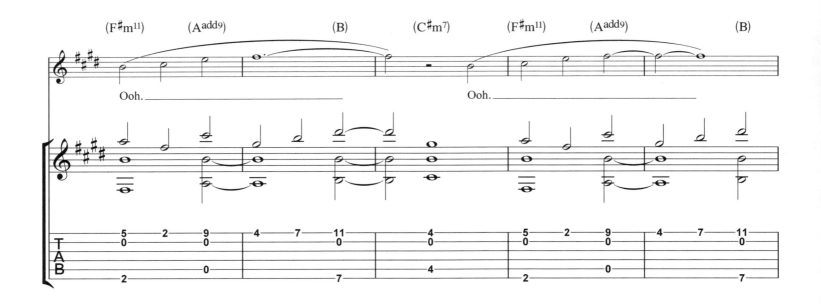

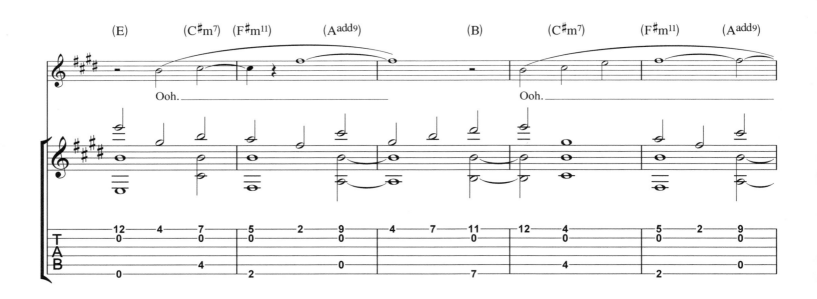

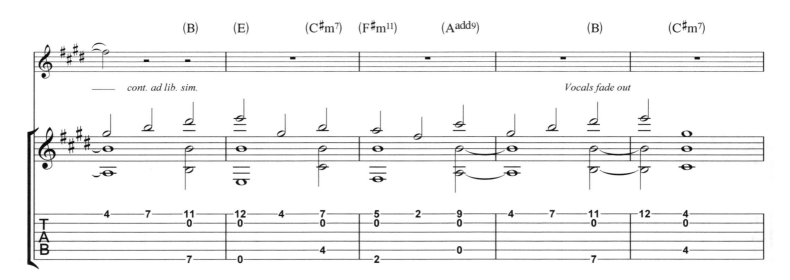

78

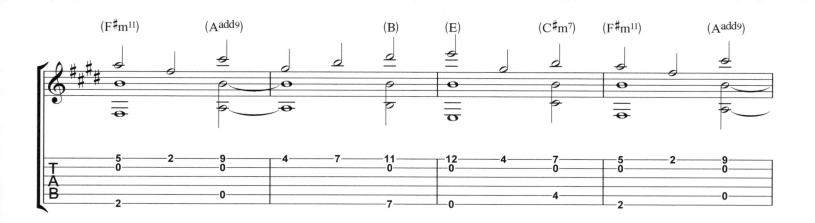

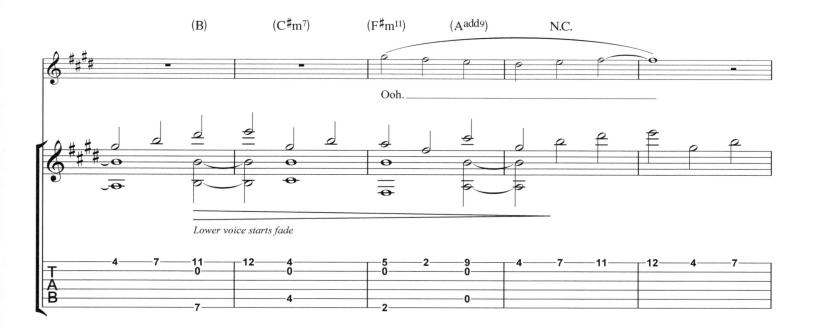

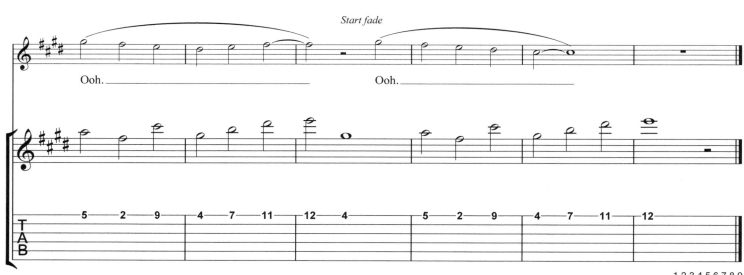

1 2 3 4 5 6 7 8 9

GUITAR TABLATURE EXPLAINED

GUITAR MUSIC CAN BE NOTATED IN THREE DIFFERENT WAYS: ON A MUSICAL STAVE, IN TABLATURE, AND IN RHYTHM SLASHES

RHYTHM SLASHES: are written above the stave. Strum chords in the rhythm indicated. Round noteheads indicate single notes.

THE MUSICAL STAVE: shows pitches and rhythms and is divided by lines into bars. Pitches are named after the first seven letters of the alphabet.

TABLATURE: graphically represents the guitar fingerboard. Each horizontal line represents a string, and each number represents a fret.

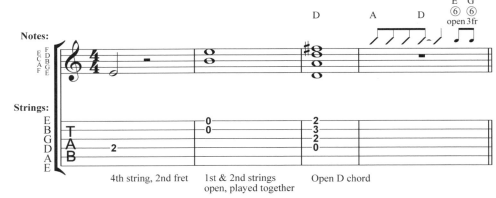

4th string, 2nd fret   1st & 2nd strings open, played together   Open D chord

DEFINITIONS FOR SPECIAL GUITAR NOTATION

SEMI-TONE BEND: Strike the note and bend up a semi-tone (½ step).

WHOLE-TONE BEND: Strike the note and bend up a whole-tone (full step).

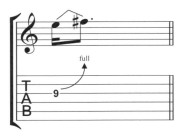

GRACE NOTE BEND: Strike the note and bend as indicated. Play the first note as quickly as possible.

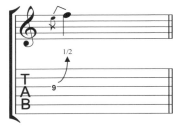

QUARTER-TONE BEND: Strike the note and bend up a ¼ step

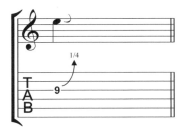

BEND & RELEASE: Strike the note and bend up as indicated, then release back to the original note.

COMPOUND BEND & RELEASE: Strike the note and bend up and down in the rhythm indicated.

PRE-BEND: Bend the note as indicated, then strike it.

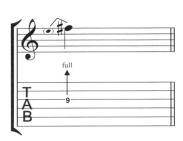

PRE-BEND & RELEASE: Bend the note as indicated. Strike it and release the note back to the original pitch.

HAMMER-ON: Strike the first note with one finger, then sound the second note (on the same string) with another finger by fretting it without picking.

PULL-OFF: Place both fingers on the note to be sounded, strike the first note and without picking, pull the finger off to sound the second note.

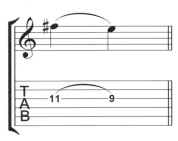

LEGATO SLIDE (GLISS): Strike the first note and then slide the same fret-hand finger up or down to the second note. The second note is not struck.

MUFFLED STRINGS: A percussive sound is produced by laying the first hand across the string(s) without depressing, and striking them with the pick hand.

NATURAL HARMONIC: Strike the note while the fret-hand lightly touches the string directly over the fret indicated.

PICK SCRAPE: The edge of the pick is rubbed down (or up) the string, producing a scratchy sound.

PALM MUTING: The note is partially muted by the pick hand lightly touching the string(s) just before the bridge.

SHIFT SLIDE (GLISS & RESTRIKE) Same as legato slide, except the second note is struck.